HOW TO SURVIVE BEING LOST AT SEA

BY SAMANTHA BELL

The Child's World®

Published by The Child's World®
1980 Lookout Drive • Mankato, MN 56003-1705
800-599-READ • www.childsworld.com

Acknowledgments
The Child's World®: Mary Berendes, Publishing Director
Red Line Editorial: Editorial direction and production
The Design Lab: Design
Photographs ©: David Wingate/Shutterstock Images, cover, 1; Shutterstock Images, 5, 17; Pat Wellenbach/AP Images, 7; Daniel Forster/AP Images, 9; Dudarev Mikhail/Shutterstock Images, 11; iStock/Thinkstock, 13; Arina Borevich/Shutterstock Images, 15; Amanda Nicholls/Shutterstock Images, 18; Sara Francis/U.S. Coast Guard/AP Images, 20

ISBN 9781609731595
LCCN 2014959920

Printed in the United States of America
Mankato, MN
July, 2015
PA02260

ABOUT THE AUTHOR

Samantha Bell lives in South Carolina with her husband, four children, and lots of animals. She has written and illustrated more than 30 books, from picture books for kids to nonfiction for older students. She loves spending time in nature but always has lots of supplies on hand.

TABLE OF CONTENTS

CHAPTER ONE

ALONE ON THE WAVES

Steve Callahan loved boats. He had dreamed of crossing the Atlantic Ocean in a small boat since he was 12 years old. That dream came true when he was 29. He and a friend crossed the ocean in the *Napoleon Solo,* which Callahan built himself.

Callahan decided to make the four-week trip back on his own. After seven days, he ran into trouble. A huge storm hit. Then, something, likely a whale, made a large hole in the side of his boat. The boat took on water fast and began to sink. He had to leave it. He inflated the *Napoleon Solo's* rubber life raft and climbed into it.

Callahan had only enough food and water on the life raft for a few days. He quickly learned how to catch fish with a spear gun. He also used a solar still. Using

Wind usually blows faster over the ocean than over land because there is less to get in its way.

sunlight, the still took the salt out of seawater. After two weeks, Callahan finally saw a ship. He set off a **flare**, but no one saw it. The ship passed by.

By day 40, the raft had ripped in one spot. Callahan kept pumping the raft's torn tube with air to keep it afloat. After ten more days, he felt like giving up. But he found a way to seal the tube using a fork and some fishing line. He had new hope.

Callahan drifted for 26 more days. His still stopped working, and he was almost out of water. But his fortune changed when he threw some fish guts into the water. Birds flew near his raft to eat the remains. Some fishermen saw the birds and rescued him. Callahan had been lost for 76 days.

HOW A SOLAR STILL WORKS

Solar stills use sunlight to turn saltwater into freshwater. Saltwater is poured into the bottom of the still, which is usually black. The dark color absorbs sunlight. Heat **evaporates** the water. Salt is left behind. The rising water vapor hits the plastic top of the still and turns into beads of water. The beads slide down the sides into a clean container. The water gathers until there is enough to drink.

Steven Callahan steers *The Clam*, a life raft he designed after being lost at sea.

Other people have been lost at sea, too. Some had the motors on their boats stop working. Other times, storms caused their boats to sink. In some cases, their boats were damaged or disabled by whales or other sea animals.

Callahan knew most boats make it safely to where they are going. He was not worried about sailing across the ocean by himself. But when something did go wrong, he knew what to do. He knew how to survive being lost at sea.

CHAPTER TWO

THE BASICS

Castaways in the middle of the ocean on a small raft must first not panic. They should calmly take time to think about their situation, then decide what to do next.

See what food, water, and equipment are available. There might be a survival kit in the raft. In 1972, Dougal Robertson, his wife, three sons, and a friend were lost at sea after a whale rammed and sank their boat. The survival kit they used had 18 pints (8.5 L) of water, some bread, fishing supplies, a signal mirror, a first-aid box, and eight flares.

Items floating in the water can help, too. If you see objects, pick them up even if they do not seem important. The Robertson family found some empty boxes, a plastic cup, and a sewing basket. Inside the

Most life rafts have kits that give people the basics for survival.

sewing basket were many more items. It had pins, string, buttons, foil, wire, aspirin, bags, a pencil, and a pen.

It is important to keep supplies safe. Items like watches and matches should be kept in waterproof containers. Tie down anything that might get washed away. Put away sharp objects that could damage the raft.

Next, consider your location. Sometimes it is best to stay where you are. If you are close to land or shipping routes, someone might find you quickly. Some people try to anchor their boat. If the survival kit does not have an anchor, you can make one. Use a bucket full of water, a heavy object, or some clothing. Tie the anchor to the end of a rope to help your raft stay in place. The Robertsons knew no one would pass by. They decided to keep drifting. After 38 days, Japanese fishermen spotted them.

If lost at sea, it may seem like there is plenty of water to drink. But you cannot drink seawater! People need to drink freshwater to survive.

Without shade from the sun, people need to drink more water to stay healthy.

Even if you have a lot of freshwater, you will want to **ration** it. Drink as little as is necessary to stay **hydrated**. People can survive on just 2.5 pints (1.2 L) of water per day. But in harsh conditions, people may need four or five times more than that. Castaways can get more water when a storm comes. Items such as plastic boxes and bags, raincoats, and boots will hold rainwater.

People who are lost at sea find ways to get enough water for amazing amounts of time. During World

War II, a Chinese sailor named Poon Lim was working on a British trading ship. A German submarine hit the trading ship and sank it. Lim escaped with just a lifejacket. After several hours, he found a wooden raft with some supplies. When his water ran out, Lim cut the canvas off of his lifejacket. He used it to collect rain. He survived on the ocean for 133 days until he was found.

In colder climates, people lost at sea might find sea ice. New sea ice is salty and cannot be used. Old sea ice has lost its salt and is a blue-gray color. You can melt this ice and drink it.

Humans can survive for weeks without food. But being lost at sea does not mean you have to go hungry.

THE EFFECTS OF DRINKING SALTWATER

If you are lost at sea and thirsty, the ocean water may look good to drink. But it will actually hurt you. Seawater is made up of many different salts. Kidneys keep the right amount of salts in the human body. This helps cells, tissues, and organs work properly. If you drink seawater, too much salt enters your body. Your kidneys cannot get rid of it. You feel even more thirsty, and your body starts to break down.

A raft's shadow may attract fish.

You might have some packaged food. You can also get your food from nature.

Fish are the main food source. But you should avoid large fish and fish with sharp teeth or **spines**. These fish could hurt you or damage the raft.

You can catch fish with fishing line, hooks, and bait. If you do not have any, you can make them with the supplies you have. Use a shoestring or sock thread for a line. A pocketknife, a piece of metal, or a wire can act as a hook. Poon Lim used the spring from a flashlight and nails from his wooden raft. Shiny objects such as jewelry or spoons can work as bait.

When people who are lost at sea catch a fish, they must decide what to do with it. Sometimes it is best to eat it right away. Without an oven, the fish must be eaten raw. If there is other food, you can save the fish for later. Cut the meat into strips and set them out on the raft to dry in the sun. That way, the meat will last longer. The other parts of the fish can be used for bait.

In 1973, Maurice and Maralyn Bailey were sailing to New Zealand when a whale struck their **yacht**, causing it to sink. On the life raft, they ate all of their food within ten days. They needed to fish but did not have any hooks, so Maralyn made her own from safety pins. She also made a trap with a can. She cut a hole in it and put bait inside. Fish swam in, and she scooped them up.

Surprising events sometimes help people survive. The Baileys caught and ate sea turtles that came by their boat. Birds landed on the raft to rest. The Baileys were able to grab the birds and eat them. Maurice and Maralyn were rescued after 117 days at sea.

Sometimes there is not much food or water available at sea. It is important to rest as much as possible when this happens. Staying awake makes you feel more hungry and thirsty.

If there are many birds around, it may mean land is near.

CHAPTER THREE

STAYING SAFE

Did you know the ocean can be a lot like a desert? The hot sun causes sunburn, **sunstroke**, and loss of fluids. When people are stuck on a raft, it is important to stay cool and hydrated.

Castaways need shelter from the sun. Many life rafts have a **canopy**. But if there is no cover, you can make one with a tarp or extra clothing. Also, try to find something to protect your eyes from the bright sunlight.

If it gets too hot during the day, you can wet your hair and clothes with seawater. You can do this as long as the salt does not irritate your skin. You can also take a dip in the ocean if the water is calm and safe.

Going up and down on the waves in a small raft makes some people **seasick**. When people are seasick,

Calm water reflects sunlight. This increases the risk of sunburn.

they may throw up a lot. Their bodies can lose a lot of valuable fluids. If you are seasick, do not eat any food until you feel better. Being sick can lead to other problems. Throwing up over the side of the raft might attract sharks.

Sharks eat fish, crabs, squid, rays, turtles, and many other sea animals. They tend to go after slow targets. If people are in the water and see a shark, they should all

There are hundreds of kinds of sharks. Most are not considered dangerous.

swim together in a large circle. Swim with strong movements if alone. That way, you will not look like a wounded animal to a shark.

The shape of clothing can confuse sharks. Keep all of your clothing on, including your shoes. But take off any jewelry. The shine from jewelry may look like a fish to sharks.

If sharks come near while castaways are in a raft, the people should be still and quiet. Bring in any fishing lines and bait that might attract the sharks. Do not let your arms and legs hang over the edge. If a shark does attack, hit it in its eyes or gills.

Poon Lim, the Robertson family, and the Baileys saw sharks while they were on their rafts. At first the survivors were afraid. But they learned how to stay safe.

Eventually, the Baileys were even able to catch and eat some smaller sharks.

Survivors should stay aware of their surroundings. Most people lost at sea are found by a passing ship, airplane, or helicopter. Some see shore and are able to land.

Groups of two or more can take turns watching for help. Help can pass by during the day or at night. If you are alone, limit the watch time to a couple hours, then

People traveling by sea can write down their plans. This helps rescuers know when something is wrong and where to start looking.

rest for a while. Dougal Robertson, his oldest son, and their friend took two-hour shifts.

Keep watching for signs of land, too. If you see a cloud in a clear sky that does not move, it is probably over land. A greenish sky is a sign of land, too. Sunlight reflects from the shallow water, making the clouds look green.

Survivors should have their signal flares ready in case they see a ship or plane. If you do not have any flares, use a pocket mirror or a cell phone screen to reflect sunlight. Movement also attracts attention. Tie brightly colored material to an oar and wave it in the air. You can use a whistle, too. Sound travels well across water. When a ship passed by the Baileys, they waved clothing. The ship turned around!

People survive being lost at sea for days, weeks, and months. It might seem that being lost for such a long period of time would make someone avoid the water. But many survivors are not afraid. Instead, they go back to the ocean, ready to travel again.

Glossary

canopy (KAN-uh-pee) A canopy is a shade or shelter. A canopy protects survivors from the heat of the sun.

castaways (KAS-tuh-wayz) Castaways are people who have been shipwrecked or stranded in an isolated place. It can be hard for castaways to find food and water.

evaporates (i-VAP-uh-rates) When water evaporates, it changes from a liquid to a gas. Ocean water evaporates in the hot sun, leaving the salt behind.

flare (flair) A flare is a device that produces a fire or blaze of light. Survivors can use a flare to signal a passing ship.

hydrated (HYE-dray-ted) When something has enough water, it is hydrated. People must be hydrated to stay healthy.

ration (RASH-uhn) To ration is to limit the amount of something used per day. People on rafts must ration supplies.

seasick (SEE-sick) Being seasick is when you feel ill from moving over waves. After days at sea, it is easy to become seasick.

spines (spines) Spines are the stiff, pointed, and sharp parts of animals. Spines help protect fish but can damage rafts.

sunstroke (SUHN-strohk) Sunstroke is an illness caused by staying in the sun for too long. People suffering from sunstroke have a high body temperature.

yacht (yaht) A yacht is a small ship used for fun or racing. Sometimes people travel long distances in a yacht.

To Learn More

BOOKS

Campbell, Guy. *The Boys' Book of Survival: How To Survive Anything, Anywhere*. New York: Scholastic, 2009.

Llewellyn, Claire. *Survive at Sea*. Charlotte: Silver Dolphin Books, 2006.

Rice, William B. *Survival! Ocean*. New York: TIME for Kids, 2012.

TIME for Kids Book of How: All About Survival. New York: TIME for Kids, 2014.

WEB SITES

Visit our Web site for links about being lost at sea:

childsworld.com/links

Note to Parents, Teachers, and Librarians: We routinely verify our Web links to make sure they are safe and active sites. So encourage your readers to check them out!

Index